STUDY GUIDE

A Survey of Church History

Part 5, AD 1800–1900

W. Robert Godfrey

LIGONIER.ORG | 800-435-4343

Copyright © 2015 Ligonier Ministries
421 Ligonier Court, Sanford, FL 32771
E-mail: info@ligonier.org
All rights reserved.
No reproduction of this work without permission.
Printed in the United States of America.

1

The Nineteenth Century

INTRODUCTION

The ideas and events of the nineteenth century produced effects that can be felt down to this day. In this introductory lesson, Dr. Godfrey shows us why the history of the church in this century still matters and gives us five categories to analyze and understand it for ourselves.

LESSON OBJECTIVES

1. To provide an overview of how the church developed in the nineteenth century
2. To establish a pattern to follow the trends of the nineteenth-century church

SCRIPTURE READING

For the word of the cross is folly to those that are perishing, but to us who are being saved it is the power of God.
—1 Corinthians 1:18

LECTURE OUTLINE

A. The nineteenth century is a rich and challenging century in church history.
   1. This series will largely focus on the American and reformed experience.
      a. The American experience was greatly influential around the world.
      b. The reformed experience was critical to the intellectual defense of the faith.
   2. This series will not be limited to the American and reformed experience.
      a. The events of this century throughout the world are still very influential on the church today.

B. The vast social and economic changes of the nineteenth century suggest that Christianity's future will be problematic.

1. Throughout this century, Christianity remains influential among common people but begins to lose its influence among cultural elites.
    a. "On Religion: Speeches to Its Cultured Despisers" is an early indication of this trend.
    b. To this day, there will be a widening gulf between a vibrant Christianity and those that despise it.
2. The French Revolution sets the stage for the nineteenth century.
    a. It showed that a violent overthrow of a monarchy and government was possible, and many Europeans wondered if other revolutions were yet to come.
    b. Napoleon is crowned as emperor of France, and the effort for democratization in the French Revolution fails as monarchies throughout Europe are strengthened.
3. The growth of cities fosters the growth of the middle class.
    a. Wealth was once based on landownership and agriculture, so people expected to remain in the class into which they were born.
    b. Colonization facilitated trade in cities, and the Industrial Revolution brought people from farms to cities with greater opportunities.
    c. Political pressures cause aristocrats and the way people see aristocrats to change.

C. There were five responses to the events in Europe during the nineteenth century.
    1. Christianity is attacked.
        a. This is a direct result of the posture of the French Revolution.
        b. There will continue to be voices attacking Christianity to the point that some will insist Christianity is dangerous.
    2. Christianity is established.
        a. There are attempts to enforce Christianity as the legal religion and to punish by law any attack against it.
        b. The establishment of Christianity is evidenced by laws of the British Parliament pardoning anyone who had served in Parliament without being a member of the Church of England.
        c. The danger is that Christianity is made the ideological prop of the government, and thus any criticism directed toward the government is directed toward Christianity
    3. Christianity is accommodated.
        a. There is a response to the growing intellectual criticism of Christianity that demands that it be accommodated to those criticisms.
        b. It is assumed that if Christianity wants to be intellectually respectable, it will have to change its attitude on the Bible and evolution.
    4. Christianity is defended.
        a. Strong intellectual defenses of the Christian faith are put forth.

    b. This is most noticeably seen through Abraham Kuyper and the Princeton theologians.
5. Christianity is revived.
    a. There is great emphasis on a vigorous commitment to Christianity in the nineteenth century.
    b. While Europe widely insists on the legal establishment of Christianity, America advances Christianity with much more success by reviving a Christianity that is vital to the heart.

STUDY QUESTIONS

1. The law stating that a person had to be a member of the Church of England in order to serve in the British Parliament an example of Christianity's being _____.
   a. Accommodated
   b. Defended
   c. Established
   d. Attacked

2. The French Revolution was successful in establishing a democracy in France.
   a. True
   b. False

3. _____ changes were the primary cause behind the attempts for democratization in the nineteenth century.
   a. Social
   b. Political
   c. Religious
   d. Economic

4. The church was not dramatically affected by the social and political changes of the nineteenth century.
   a. True
   b. False

5. Which of the following did not lead to the rise of the middle class in the nineteenth century?
   a. The Industrial Revolution
   b. The ownership of land
   c. The growth of cities
   d. The increase in trade

6. In the nineteenth century, that the Bible was beginning to be viewed in light of evolutionary theory is an example of Christianity's being _____.
   a. Attacked
   b. Revived
   c. Accommodated
   d. Established

DISCUSSION QUESTIONS

1. What is different about the attempts to revive Christianity in America as compared to the attempts made in Europe during the nineteenth century?

2. What are the similarities of the French Revolution's attack on Christianity and today's attacks on Christianity?

3. What can you imagine are some of the dangers of establishing Christianity by law?

4. Why is the reformed experience so important to emphasize throughout the course of nineteenth-century church history?

2

The Intellectual Scene

INTRODUCTION

Ideas have consequences, and the intellectual changes that were taking place in Europe would set the stage for the entire nineteenth century. In this lesson, Dr. Godfrey explores those ideas and how they began to expand beyond the continent of Europe and influence American religious life.

LESSON OBJECTIVES

1. To overview the intellectual climate of Europe in the nineteenth century
2. To recognize important European thinkers
3. To outline the parallel developments in America

SCRIPTURE READING

The one who states his case first seems right, until the other comes and examines him.

—Proverbs 18:17

Where were you when I laid the foundation of the earth?

—Job 38:4a

LECTURE OUTLINE

A. Intellectual changes were taking place in the nineteenth century.
   1. The thought outside the church is becoming the dominant way of thinking, and the church must decide how it will react.
      a. These changes mark the beginnings of liberal theology.
      b. They are important to note because they are informative for the exchange between the church and culture today.

B. Europe was leaving the Enlightenment behind.
   1. The Enlightenment inspired confidence in the autonomy of reason, and the freedom and dignity of man became foundational to Enlightenment thought.
   2. It was believed that a life freed from the Bible and from Christianity was not only better but also possible.
   3. This confidence in the ability of reason to reach universal principles for all of mankind was soon questioned.
   4. David Hume, one of the Enlightenment's most important thinkers, was already introducing a new skepticism as to the actual capabilities of reason.

C. European thinkers began to use different categories to understand reality.
   1. Reason remains an important authority for interpreting the world, but it will no longer be thought of as capable of the task by itself.
   2. Experience becomes an important criterion of understanding.
      a. Experience in this sense should be understood as feelings.
      b. It is no longer our reasoning about what is right but also our feelings about what is right that guides us.
      c. This gives birth to the Romantic Movement.
   3. History is beginning to be taken seriously in the nineteenth century.
      a. History becomes a key element to understanding humanity, religion, and truth.
      b. It is the combination of reason, experience, and history that makes way for the accommodation of Christianity to the criticisms against it.
      c. As Christians who place our trust in the Bible, we ultimately see the Bible as transcending culture, experience, and reason.

D. European thinkers challenged elements of the Bible and received Christian truth.
   1. Immanuel Kant was an astute philosopher of the late eighteenth century.
      a. He believed that the most essential aspect of religion is morality—that which we ought to do.
      b. Morality becomes primary over truth.
   2. Hegel was an important thinker of the nineteenth century who stressed the movement of history as foundational to his philosophy.
      a. He believed that if history is always moving, it is always changing, and so our understanding of truth is always changing.
      b. What we understand to be true (thesis) meets a contrary point of view (antithesis) and there is mediating position that is reached (synthesis). This process of synthesis continues forever.
      c. The Hegelian notion of the movement of history influenced many thinkers.
         i. Karl Marx made this foundational for communism.
         ii. Ferdinand Christian Baur made this his approach to the Bible.

    d. Hegel insisted that his thought was based on reason, but it challenged the simplicity of truth, which challenges the Christian faith.
  3. Friedrich Schleiermacher is a notable theologian of the nineteenth century.
    a. He believed experience and feeling to be at the heart of Christianity.
    b. He genuinely believed that he was defending the Christian faith, but to make feelings the basis for truth is just a product of an Enlightenment optimism that ignores revelation.

E. American religious life was changing.
  1. America was also being influenced by the optimism that was changing European thought.
  2. In Europe there was an attack on Christianity generally, but in America there was an attack on Calvinism specifically.
    a. Up until the nineteenth century, Calvinism was the dominant religious expression in America.
    b. Calvinism was beginning to be seen as excessively pessimistic, and as the frontiers of America expanded, it was left behind.
  3. Methodists and Baptists became the largest denominations in America.

STUDY QUESTIONS

1. David Hume was an Enlightenment philosopher who promoted the trustworthiness and universality of reason.
    a. True
    b. False

2. Immanuel Kant believed _____ was the primary purpose of religion.
    a. Spirituality
    b. Authenticity
    c. Rationality
    d. Morality

3. Which of the following is not a key component to Hegel's thought?
    a. Synthesis
    b. Antithesis
    c. Metathesis
    d. Thesis

4. Who is the most important thinker influenced by Hegel?
    a. Ferdinand Christian Baur
    b. Karl Marx
    c. Immanuel Kant
    d. Friedrich Schleiermacher

5. Schleiermacher believed that Christianity was essentially feeling and experience.
    a. True
    b. False

6. What will be the result of Enlightenment optimism in America during the nineteenth century?
    a. An attack on Calvinism
    b. A suspicion of education
    c. Methodist and Baptist prominence
    d. All of the above

DISCUSSION QUESTIONS

1. Understanding the intellectual changes taking place in the nineteenth century helps us understand that the church cannot live in absolute separation from the world. What are the important cultural trends influencing—and perhaps threatening—the church today?

2. The emphasis placed on history for a proper understanding of humanity was a key element of nineteenth-century thought. How should that shape our approach to the Bible?

3. Schleiermacher genuinely thought he was defending Christianity by stressing the centrality of feeling in evaluating religion. Can you identify the main problem with Schleiermacher's idea?

4. While intellectuals in Europe were becoming critical of Christianity in general, why was Calvinism specifically targeted in America?

3

Two American Revolutions

INTRODUCTION

The American Revolution and the Second American Revolution will have a significant impact on the development of the church in America. In this lesson, Dr. Godfrey explains how these revolutions made the churches in America different from the churches in Europe and led to the Second Awakening.

LESSON OBJECTIVES

1. To show how the American Revolutions shaped American religious life
2. To consider the factors leading up to the prominence of Methodist and Baptist denominations in America
3. To introduce the Second Awakening

SCRIPTURE READING

And he made from one man every nation of mankind to live on the face of the earth, having determined and allotted periods and the boundaries of their dwelling places.

—Acts 17:26

LECTURE OUTLINE

A. The American Revolution must be considered in order to understand the nineteenth-century American experience.

  1. Men of wealth, education, and property led the American Revolution, and they did not aim to radically change the established order.
     a. They aimed to preserve the rights of Englishmen in America by way of preserving the established order from English interference.
     b. The king's interference, taxation without representation, and threats to American religious freedom made way for the American Revolution.

2. The revolution had a profound impact on churches in America.
    a. The federal government would not establish a church by law.
    b. This freedom of religion meant that all denominations would be treated equally under law.

B. Denominationalism is the dominant expression of the American religious experience.
    1. Denominationalism is the idea that the Christian church finds expression in a variety of organizations.
    2. It allows Christians to be separated over certain points while acknowledging that, at the fundamental level, we are all still Christians.
        a. This is a radical development in church history that primarily takes place in the nineteenth century.
    3. Denominationalism affords Christians the opportunity to cooperate in fundamental ways like evangelism, missions, and education.

C. Voluntarism is necessary for American churches to survive.
    1. There is a fundamental difference between churches in Europe and churches in America during the nineteenth century.
        a. In Europe, the government built churches and paid ministers.
        b. In America, the government did not establish a religion, so if churches were to exist, Americans would have to pay for them.
    2. There is a vitality in American churches that is missing from European churches in the nineteenth century.
        a. In Europe, a minister gets paid regardless of how little he cares for his people.
        b. In America, there is a more intimate relationship between the people and their minister.
            i. If the pews are empty, a minister will not be able to make a living while fulfilling his call.
            ii. A potential downfall is the danger that a minister may accommodate his message to his people's thinking.
        c. In America, people felt truly connected to their church and wanted to be involved in it.

D. The Second American Revolution also helps us to understand the nineteenth-century American experience.
    1. The First American Revolution was a revolution that ensured the elites would maintain a significant influence on how the country would be governed.
    2. The Second American Revolution was the growing conviction that the government ought to be more popularly controlled.
    3. The Second American Revolution gave more power to the common people, and the influence of Methodists and Baptists grew.

E. Methodists and Baptists would become the largest denominations in America.
   1. Methodists and Baptists could immediately appeal to common people in America.
      a. The educational standards of Methodists and Baptists were low, so they were able to speak in a language familiar to most people.
      b. As people moved west, an educated clergy seemed less significant.
   2. Methodists and Baptists were willing to move into the difficult conditions of the west.
      a. America's population was booming. The pressures of a growing population drove people west in search of new farmland.
      b. People lived on large farms and were so isolated from each other that the prospect of churches and schools was difficult to imagine.
      c. Methodists and Baptists were willing to meet the demands of these living conditions.
         i. Methodists developed circuit riders who would preach in one village on a Sunday and another village on the next.
         ii. Camp meetings were developed to get people together for a concentrated time of religious experience.

F. The Second Great Awakening marks a period of significant development for the church during the early nineteenth century.
   1. The camp meeting at Cane Ridge in 1801 was one of the landmark events of the Second Great Awakening.
      a. It is estimated that 25,000 people attended and a huge revival occurred.
      b. There were physical manifestations of what people believed was the presence and power of the Holy Spirit.
   2. The Second Great Awakening lasted longer than the First Great Awakening, but it was not as spiritually intense.
      a. The Second Great Awakening lasted from approximately 1800 to 1830–35.
      b. The Second Awakening brought people back into the churches by making church membership more accessible.
         i. Methodist and Baptist preachers stressed an immediate response to Christ.
         ii. In many ways, this was a reaction against Calvinism.
      c. The Second Great Awakening would have a huge impact on the development of religion in America.

STUDY QUESTIONS

1. The First American Revolution had a profound effect on the rise of _____ in America.
   a. Presbyterianism
   b. Denominationalism
   c. Evangelism
   d. Fundamentalism

2. The idea that if churches are going to exist, then we will have to pay for them is called denominationalism.
   a. True
   b. False

3. The growing desire for democratization in America has been called the _____.
   a. First American Revolution
   b. First Great Awakening
   c. Second American Revolution
   d. Second Great Awakening

4. Education seemed less significant to the people who were expanding the American frontier.
   a. True
   b. False

5. What solution was offered for the many difficulties that hindered the life of the church on the frontier?
   a. Methodist circuit riders
   b. Camp meetings
   c. Farm churches
   d. Both a and b

6. The _____ revival in 1801 typically marks the beginning of the Second Great Awakening.
   a. Gasper River
   b. Cumberland
   c. Cane Ridge
   d. Red River

DISCUSSION QUESTIONS

1. What important improvements did denominationalism offer to the churches in nineteenth-century America?

2. What were the positive outcomes of the development of voluntarism in America? What continues to be the potential downside?

3. What factors contributed to the rapid growth of the Baptist and Methodist denominations in America?

4. Why was the Second Great Awakening so successful in bringing large numbers of people back into American churches?

4

The Second Awakening

INTRODUCTION

The Second Great Awakening was a period of increased evangelism and social reform. In this lesson, Dr. Godfrey explains how the Second Great Awakening would influence society and introduces its important theologians.

LESSON OBJECTIVES

1. To present the Second Great Awakening as a period of revitalization and dramatic change
2. To explore the influence of Calvinistic preachers and evangelists during the Second Great Awakening
3. To introduce the life and theology of Charles Finney

SCRIPTURE READING

Will you not revive us again, that your people may rejoice in you?

—Psalm 85:6

LECTURE OUTLINE

A. The Second Great Awakening was a period in church history where American religion was revived, renewed, and radically changed.
   1. It was a period of increased evangelicalism.
      a. It is called the beginning of the Evangelical Empire in America.
      b. Churches became committed to missions and educational programs and experienced increased evangelical success.
   2. It was a period of social reform.
      a. Specialized societies and rescue missions addressed issues including dueling, Freemasonry, prostitution, and slavery.

  b. Between 1810 and 1820, the American Protestant attitude toward alcohol changed, and the vast majority of Americans turned against alcohol.
 3. It was a period of democratized Christianity.
  a. Americans in general began to hold expert opinion as suspect.
   i. Americans began to question doctors and lawyers.
   ii. Health food movements began in this period.
  b. Likewise, educated ministers and theologians were called into question.
   i. People believed that theologians were unnecessary to understand the Bible.
   ii. It was thought that people should therefore make the important decisions about religion without them.

B. Calvinist preachers still had a considerable impact during the Second Great Awakening.
 1. Asahel Nettleton was a prominent Calvinistic preacher in the early nineteenth century.
  a. He represented the continuing tradition of influential Calvinistic preachers, evangelists, and church builders.
  b. He was known for his preaching, which led to conversions and church-planting efforts throughout the country.
 2. Lyman Beecher was another prominent Calvinistic preacher of the early nineteenth century.
  a. He was born and educated in Connecticut.
  b. He moved to Ohio under the conviction that the West would shape the future of the country.
  c. Beecher's *A Plea for the West* urged young preachers to move west.
   i. Beecher believed that Unitarianism and Roman Catholicism were the greatest dangers America faced.
   ii. He believed the greatest need in order to bring about revival in America was to stop them both.
  d. Beecher had two very influential children.
   i. Harriet Beecher Stowe would write *Uncle Tom's Cabin* as an emotional appeal against slavery.
   ii. Henry Ward Beecher would become one of the most famous preachers in America, but he was primarily influenced by liberal theology.

C. Charles Finney was the most influential theologian of the Second Awakening.
 1. He lived a long and influential life from 1792 to 1875.
  a. He was born in Connecticut and raised in New York.
  b. He was originally a lawyer and later become a Presbyterian minister.
   i. He never went to school for theology.
   ii. Finney did not place any priority on education but was primarily concerned with communicating effectively.

4—The Second Awakening

   c. He labored in a part of western New York that had so much religious activity and fervency that it was known as "the Burned-Over District."
      i. This area of New York would later produce Joseph Smith and William Miller.
   d. Finney would eventually leave Presbyterianism behind.
2. Finney developed a theology that can be best understood by looking at his most popular works.
   a. Finney's *Lectures on Revival* was written as a manual for revivals and how to promote them.
      i. Finney believed that a revival was simply a faithful work of men that could be achieved through prayers in faith.
      ii. This is at odds with the Calvinistic view that revivals are a miraculous and supernatural work of the Holy Spirit.
   b. Finney's *Systematic Theology* reveals how antagonistic he had become toward Calvinism.
      i. Finney was consistently Pelagian.
      ii. He taught that anyone who preaches that you are saved by the imputed righteousness of Christ preaches a false gospel.
      iii. He taught that in order to be saved you must be entirely consecrated to Christ.
3. Finney had a huge impact on American revivalism.
   a. He is within the "Apostolic" tradition of evangelists in America that some Protestant circles believe attests to the faithfulness of the American church.
      i. The succession flows from George Whitefield to Charles Finney to Dwight Moody to Billy Sunday to Billy Graham.
   b. Finney made American revivalism distinctly Arminian with his introduction of "new measures" for religious experience.
      i. Finney believed God worked through excitement—an idea that would have great impact on the church.

STUDY QUESTIONS

1. Both Lyman Beecher and Charles Finney were faithful Calvinistic preachers of the early nineteenth century.
   a. True
   b. False

2. Lyman Beecher believed that Roman Catholicism and _____ were the greatest threats to American religion.
   a. Seventh-Day Adventism
   b. Jehovah's Witnesses
   c. Unitarianism
   d. Mormonism

3. Which influential figures did "the Burned-Over District" of western New York produce?
   a. Joseph Smith
   b. William Miller
   c. Charles Finney
   d. All of the above

4. Charles Finney was able to communicate effectively because of his education in theology.
   a. True
   b. False

5. Charles Finney is one of the most consistent _____ in church history.
   a. Preterists
   b. Socinians
   c. Nestorians
   d. Pelagians

6. The idea that the faithfulness of the American church is evident by a line of faithful evangelists is called the _____ of evangelists in America.
   a. Apostolic succession
   b. Apostolic tradition
   c. Apostolic lineage
   d. Apostolic seed

DISCUSSION QUESTIONS

1. The democratization of Christianity in America during the nineteenth century lead to an excessive distrust of expert authority. What are some of the dangers of this kind of an attitude?

2. Considering the life of Charles Finney, what could be one of the reasons his theology strayed so far from the historic Protestant tradition?

3. In what ways did Charles Finney preach a different gospel?

4. What is the main similarity between Finney's beliefs about how to bring about revival and Arminian theology?

5

Charles Finney

INTRODUCTION

Charles Finney believed revival could be broken down to a science. In this lesson, Dr. Godfrey introduces Finney's methods, his many critics, and the nature of true revival.

LESSON OBJECTIVES

1. To enumerate Finney's new measures for revival
2. To voice the criticism of Finney's contemporaries

SCRIPTURE READING

Other seeds fell on rocky ground, where they did not have much soil, and immediately they sprang up, since they had no depth of soil.
—Matthew 13:5

LECTURE OUTLINE

A. Charles Finney warned the church about the nature of excitement.
   1. He believed excitement was necessary for the growth and development of the church and would be necessary up until Christ's millennial reign.
   2. He was a strong postmillennialist who believed the millennium would have to come soon.
      a. He believed the church cannot handle a long period of excitement, so if the church requires excitement, then the millennium must be soon.
   3. Finney warned that the church would break down just like an endlessly excited nervous system would break down.
   4. Finney was actually right, and despite this, he is still influential in leading the church to seek out the new and exciting to this day.

B. Finney's new measures were the controversial means by which he attempted to induce conversion.

1. He allowed women to preach in mixed audiences.
    a. This was a day when if a woman were to pray in public in the company of men, let alone preach, it would be shocking.
2. He introduced protracted meetings.
    a. Instead of moving on to another town after a night of preaching, Finney would stay in a town and preach again the next night.
        i. This could last for up to two weeks.
    b. Finney believed these meetings built the excitement and anticipation of the crowd.
3. He used methods to break down barriers between himself and the crowd.
    a. He used colloquial language.
        i. Many objected that his language simply did not match the dignity of the gospel.
    b. He would pray for the unconverted by name.
    c. He would allow people to become church members immediately upon conversion.
4. Finney's most controversial new measure was "the anxious bench."
    a. Finney would keep a bench open at the front of the church while he preached.
    b. He would ask people who were feeling spiritually anxious to move forward and sit on the bench so he could preach directly to them.
    c. This is the beginning of what would come to be known as "the altar call."

C. John Williamson Nevin strongly objected to Finney's anxious bench.
    1. Nevin believed that American Protestantism faced two choices.
        a. The church could follow Finney's use of the anxious bench.
            i. If this case, Christianity is merely about excitement and sudden conversions.
            ii. Nevin believed that the whole idea of going forward to the anxious bench distracted a person from the spiritual reality of giving his life to Christ.
        b. The church could hold to the faith as expressed in her catechisms.
            i. If this case, Christianity is about the maturity and growth of the believer.
            ii. Nevin loved the Heidelberg Catechism and believed it would lead Christians to a gradual, full maturity in the faith.
    2. In spite of such objections, Finney was very successful.
        a. He worked hard.
        b. He was optimistic in an age of optimism.
        c. He preached powerfully.
        d. He connected with common people.

D. Charles Finney's theology and methodology would continue to be critiqued by notable theologians.
    1. Finney would himself remark that the people who were affected by his ministry were not persevering in the faith.

2. Charles Hodge made some very penetrating critiques of Finney.
   a. Finney's emphasis on the sinner's choosing God made no reference to Christ as the one mediator between God and man.
   b. Finney's method did not communicate God's method of salvation.
   c. Finney's theology resembled the developing German liberal theology and its view of God.
3. B.B. Warfield wrote extensively about Charles Finney.
   a. Finney could entirely leave God out because he only created a system of morals.
4. John Williamson Nevin further critiqued Finney in his reflections on the nature of revival.
   a. Nevin stressed the ordinary means of grace.
   b. Revival is to be understood as God's sending the Holy Spirit to grant a special blessing on those ordinary means of grace.
   c. Finney departed from these ordinary means of grace.
5. Mark Twain even commented on the nature of revivalism in America.
   a. During an episode in *The Adventures of Tom Sawyer*, Twain notes how quickly a revival can sweep through a town and how just as quickly people can fall away.

E. Dwight L. Moody succeeded Charles Finney in the history of revivalism in America.
   1. Moody was in many ways different from Finney.
      a. Moody preached extensively on God's love.
      b. He did not consider himself a theologian.
   2. Moody was also similar to Finney.
      a. He worked hard to speak about and lead people to Christ.
   3. Moody was a very influential evangelist.
      a. He wanted to communicate the essentials of the gospel.
         i. People criticized him for being a reductionist.
      b. He would encourage American Protestants to embrace a premillennial eschatology.
         i. He was highly influential during the prophecy conferences that played a role in the growth of dispensational premillennialism.
         ii. The widespread embrace of premillennialism was a clear indication of a growing pessimism.

STUDY QUESTIONS

1. Charles Finney believed that protracted meetings helped lead to conversion through _____.
   a. Social pressure
   b. Excitement
   c. Ingenuity
   d. Anxiety

2. Charles Finney's protracted meetings were the precursor to the altar call.
   a. True
   b. False

3. A prominent criticism of Finney's approach concerned the _____ of his converts.
   a. Repentance
   b. Assurance
   c. Perseverance
   d. All of the above

4. Charles Finney is accused of preaching another gospel because he had a low view of _____.
   a. Christ
   b. Sin
   c. Man
   d. Both a and b

5. True revival does not take place apart from the _____.
   a. Holy Spirit
   b. Preaching of the gospel
   c. Administration of the sacraments
   d. All of the above

6. Dwight L. Moody influenced the spread of _____ in American Protestantism.
   a. Postmillennialism
   b. Premillennialism
   c. Amillennialism
   d. None of the above

DISCUSSION QUESTIONS

1. Charles Finney's most controversial new measure was the anxious bench. Explain and evaluate the many criticisms against this novel practice.

2. Explain and evaluate John Williamson Nevin's critique of Charles Finney's theology and practice.

3. What was attributed as the main reason for Finney's success? What should we learn from this?

6

The Rise of Cults in America

INTRODUCTION

Cults flourished in America during the nineteenth century. In this lesson, Dr. Godfrey explores where these cults came from, who started them, what they taught, and why they are so dangerous.

LESSON OBJECTIVES

1. To classify the cults of nineteenth-century America into four major categories
2. To introduce their unique origins and heretical teachings

SCRIPTURE READING

But even if we or an angel from heaven should preach to you a gospel contrary to the one we preached to you, let him be accursed.
—Galatians 1:8

They went out from us, but they were not of us; for if they had been of us, they would have continued with us.
—1 John 2:19a

LECTURE OUTLINE

A. Cults developed alongside the nineteenth-century revivalist movements in America.
  1. Cults are groups that stray from the received truth of Christianity.
     a. They can go so far as to reject the essential doctrines of God or the doctrines of Christ.
  2. America has been the most productive source of cults in church history.
     a. America has enjoyed a considerable amount of religious freedom.
     b. Without any legal restrictions to religious practice, a religious group would have to be breaking the law for the government to intervene.
        i. A good example of this can be found in early Mormonism.

ii. It was only when Mormons changed their view on polygamy that Utah was granted statehood.
3. There are four types and characteristics of the cults that developed in America during the nineteenth century.

B. Restorationist cults teach that true Christianity was lost at some time in the past and is now being restored.
1. Mormonism is an example of a restorationist cult.
    a. Joseph Smith taught that Christianity had been lost, and now that the prophetic office was restored, the true practice of Christianity was restored.
    b. Mormonism claims that it alone is the representation of the true church.

C. Healing cults teach that certain religious practices can lead to healing.
1. People were skeptical of the limited knowledge of doctors and yet at the same time were open to claims of healing.
2. Christian Science is the most famous healing cult of the nineteenth century.
    a. Mary Baker Eddy founded the Christian Science movement.
    b. The emphasis on healing ties in with the emphasis on spirituality.

D. Spirituality cults teach a new and fresh take on practicing religion and understanding the presence and power of God.
1. Christian Science was also a prominent spirituality cult.
    a. Eddy combined a new approach to spirituality that she claimed would lead to healing.
2. Christian Science is very different from Mormonism is this respect.
    a. Mormonism is a cult almost entirely focused on the physical.
        i. It views the physical aspects of temple obligations, marriage, and family as feeding into the next life.
        ii. It places the physical in such a high regard that it distorts God's true nature.
        iii. It even teaches that we can all become gods.
    b. Christian Science is a cult almost entirely focused on the spiritual.
        i. It teaches that physical reality is the illusion of evil forces controlling your mind.
        ii. It teaches that being freed from the illusion would free someone from sickness, pain, and death.
        iii. It is only a matter of thinking properly.
3. What is the attraction to these cults and their teachings?
    a. People are naturally attracted to an emphasis that is placed on either the physical or the spiritual aspects of life.
    b. Powerful charismatic leaders attract people to these cults.

    i. Joseph Smith and Brigham Young were the first charismatic leaders of Mormonism, and Mary Baker Eddy is the most prominent figure in Christian Science.
    ii. They were all effective communicators who were driven by their own vision.
  c. American Protestants were content not to have education or a real theological system.
    i. Gullibility fuels cults, because cults prey on the susceptibility of people.
    ii. When cults twist Scripture, people think they are being enlightened; in actuality, they are being deceived.
  d. It is demonic strategy that ultimately leads people away from the truth.

E. Eschatology cults teach the imminence of Christ's return, an expectation that controls the rest of the worldview.
  1. William Miller is very important to the rise of eschatology cults in nineteenth century America.
    a. He was from the Burned-Over District in western New York.
    b. He believed he had discovered the date of Christ's return.
      i. He first set a date in 1843 and then another in October 1844.
      ii. People sold their property in preparation for Christ's return.
      iii. The failure of Miller's second prophecy became known as "the Great Disappointment."
  2. Miller greatly influenced eschatology cults like Jehovah's Witnesses and Seventh-day Adventists.
    a. Ellen G. White would reinterpret "the Great Disappointment" as Christ's invisible return to glory.
      i. Christ entered into the heavenly temple and began the investigative judgment to determine who would finally enter the eternal kingdom.
    b. The followers of Ellen G. White began Seventh-day Adventism.
      i. Seventh-day Adventism is still driven by the eschatological expectation of Christ's return.
      ii. Seventh-day Adventism is less cultic than when it first began.
      iii. It is still very adamant that Saturday is the day that Christians ought to keep holy.
  3. The Shakers are a cult inspired by Mother Ann Less Stanley.
    a. Mother Ann Lee Stanley was a part of the Quaker movement.
      i. She became a prominent figure and developed a following that worshiped so ecstatically that they became known as Shakers.
    b. Stanley taught that Christ would return as a woman, and proper preparation for Christ's return involved celibate communities governed by millennial laws.

                i. People would leave their spouses to become part of the community, or they would join the community with their spouses but remain celibate.
                ii. Men and women lived separately.
            c. The Shakers flourished between 1830 and 1850.
                i. They lived simply and made furniture to support the community.
                ii. Speaking in tongues and dancing were characteristic of Shaker worship.
                iii. Dancing was considered to be a form of spiritual humility.

    F. In nineteenth-century America, there were many voices that claimed to be biblical in interest of bringing restoration, healing, true spirituality, and proper expectation to the church.
        1. How is it that so many people were lead astray?
            a. Sometimes people have a desire to be the only ones who really know the truth.
                i. Cults have always claimed that they alone are going to get into heaven.
                ii. Calvinism has never had such extreme exclusivity.

STUDY QUESTIONS

1. The belief that Joseph Smith was the rebirth of a long-lost line of prophets makes Mormonism a _____ cult.
    a. Eschatology
    b. Healing
    c. Restorationist
    d. Spirituality

2. Christian Science was founded by _____.
    a. Mother Ann Lee Stanley
    b. Mary Baker Eddy
    c. Ellen G. White
    d. None of the above

3. Christian Science is like Mormonism in its emphasis on the physical aspects of religion.
    a. True
    b. False

4. William Miller influenced the _____ cults of the nineteenth century.
    a. Restorationist
    b. Healing
    c. Spirituality
    d. Eschatology

5. The failed anticipation of Christ's return in October 1844 is known as the
   _____.
   a. Great Disillusionment
   b. Investigative Judgment
   c. Invisible Return of Christ
   d. Great Disappointment

6. Tongues and ecstatic dancing are the focal point of Quaker worship.
   a. True
   b. False

DISCUSSION QUESTIONS

1. Why has America acted as such fertile soil for cults to grow and flourish?
2. What are the radical implications of Mormonism's emphasis on the physical in relation to the nature of God?
3. How did the suspicion of expert opinion during the nineteenth century lead to the rise of cults in America?
4. Unlike many of the cults mentioned in this lecture, the Shakers were unable to survive. To what do you ascribe this?

7

The Presbyterian Witness

INTRODUCTION

The Presbyterian church experienced the revival that swept across America by balancing the desire for vital religion with the desire for sound theology. In this lesson, Dr. Godfrey explains why this was a critical process in the development of the Presbyterian church during nineteenth-century America.

LESSON OBJECTIVES

1. To provide a history of the Presbyterian church in America
2. To show the influence of revivalism on the Presbyterian church

SCRIPTURE READING

But all things should be done decently and in order.

—1 Corinthians 14:40

For though I am absent in body, yet I am with you in spirit, rejoicing the see your good order and the firmness of your faith in Christ.

—Colossians 2:5b

LECTURE OUTLINE

A. The history of American Presbyterianism helps us understand its unique perspective on revivalism as it swept the nation.
   1. Scots-Irish immigrants founded the Presbyterian church during the eighteenth century.
      a. William Penn, the founder of Pennsylvania, encouraged Scots-Irish immigration.
         i. Penn was a Quaker and pacifist.
         ii. He invited the Scots-Irish to protect the southeast border of Pennsylvania.

2. The Presbyterian church would soon become large enough to organize itself.
   a. It formed a presbytery.
   b. It was soon able to organize a general assembly
   c. It adopted a book of church order and the Westminster Standards.
      i. In the American context, exceptions were allowed concerning the Westminster Confession of Faith's teaching that the magistrate must support the true church.
      ii. This small area of exception would open up into the larger question of the degree to which ministers and elders could take exceptions to the confession.
3. Presbyterians reconstructed the church as it existed in Scotland or Northern Ireland.
   a. They only sang psalms, and there were no musical instruments.
   b. The Great Awakening would introduce hymns into churches, and organs would soon to follow after.

B. American Presbyterianism began to change because of the influence of revivalism.
   1. Presbyterians have a unique angle on revivalism in America.
      a. Presbyterians understand the importance of a vital religion.
      b. Presbyterians also understand that there are aspects of the faith that do not just come and go.
   2. Presbyterians needed to determine what were wise accommodations to the rapidly changing culture.
      a. The great emphasis in America during the nineteenth century was on revival and the growth of the church.
      b. What place should the unique Reformed doctrines in the Westminster Confession have in this period of revival and growth?
   3. Presbyterians divided into two camps based on how the church should approach revival.
      a. The Old School wanted distinctly Presbyterian organization to support the efforts for revival.
      b. The New School wanted to downplay Presbyterian distinctives in order to cooperate with other denominations.
      c. It is important to note that both sides were pro-revival, unlike the Old Side/New Side split during the eighteenth century.
   4. The Plan of Union in 1801 further complicated issues between the Old School and the New School.
      a. The Plan of Union in 1801 was enacted in order to promote cooperation between Presbyterians and Congregationalists in expanding the church on the frontier.
         i. Evangelism efforts were divided between Congregationalists to the north and Presbyterians to the south.
         ii. Once churches were established, they could then decide to be Presbyterian or Congregationalist.

b. Theology was changing faster in Congregational churches than it was in Presbyterian churches.
   i. Revivalism was influencing Congregationalists in a way that their theology sounded Arminian to Presbyterians.
c. The Old School was very concerned that under the Plan of Union, Congregationalist ministers could freely enter the Presbyterian church without being examined.

C. The tension over revivalism began to threaten a split in the Presbyterian church.
1. The Old School and the New School had different concerns about what was happening in the Presbyterian church.
   a. The Old School worried that Presbyterian doctrine was being diluted.
   b. The New School charged the Old School with undermining evangelism.
2. The New School would consistently be in the majority at the general assembly for some years.
   a. This continued to increase tensions between the Old School and New School.
   b. Princeton Seminary did not want a war in the church and so attempted to moderate Old School frustrations.
      i. It is important to note that Princeton was Old School in its commitments.
3. The Old School finally had the majority during the general assembly of 1837.
   a. Old School ministers ended the Union of 1801 by removing four synods of churches founded under the Union.
   b. This is considered one of the most dramatic moments in the history of American Presbyterianism.
4. The New School planned to seize control of general assembly in 1838 to reverse the decision.
   a. The Old School heard about the plan and arrived early to the general assembly.
   b. The moderator did not call the roll for the representatives of the excised synod.
   c. The New School marched out to form its own general assembly.
5. There would be two Presbyterian churches in America with the same name from 1838 to 1869.
   a. The New School would not grow as quickly as the Old School.
      i. The Old School had strong leadership and the support of Princeton Seminary.

D. There still remained tensions within the Old School after the split.
1. Slavery was becoming a divisive issue in America.
   a. The South believed that slavery should be maintained.
   b. The North believed that slavery should be abolished.

2. The general assembly of 1818 issued a strong statement in opposition to slavery.
   a. It used the word "abolition" before the word became known as the technical term for the immediate end of slavery.
   b. It was not a controversial statement for Southern Presbyterians.
      i. The invention of the cotton gin would make the South more dependent on slavery after the general assembly's statement of 1818.
   c. The general assembly's statement has never been revoked.
3. The Civil War would soon divide the country and the churches between North and South.
   a. Methodist, Baptist, and Presbyterian denominations split.

STUDY QUESTIONS

1. American Presbyterians were all very resistant to the introduction of hymns and musical instruments to worship.
   a. True
   b. False

2. The Plan of Union in 1801 was between the Presbyterian church and the _____.
   a. Baptists
   b. Methodists
   c. Congregationalists
   d. All of the above

3. Princeton Seminary was largely sympathetic to the cause of New School Presbyterians.
   a. True
   b. False

4. The Old School _____ four synods of Plan of Union churches at the general assembly of 1837.
   a. Removed
   b. Excised
   c. Detached
   d. Assimilated

5. The term _____ was used by the General Assembly in 1818 before it was more popularly used throughout America.
   a. Excised
   b. Abolition
   c. Prohibition
   d. Both a and b

6. The _____ further divided the North and the South over slavery.
   a. Abolitionists
   b. General assembly of 1818
   c. Cotton gin
   d. Plan of Union

DISCUSSION QUESTIONS

1. How was the Presbyterian Church's approach to revivalism different from the approach of other American denominations?

2. How can you use the history of division within the American Presbyterian church to emphasize the importance of the Reformed tradition?

3. The New School accused the Old School of being against the growth of the church. How is this a false accusation?

4. It is common today for the Bible to be ridiculed over the issue of slavery. Appealing to church history, use the 1818 general assembly's statement to answer this oft-repeated, misguided attack.

8

Through the Civil War

INTRODUCTION

The Civil War not only divided the nation, it divided the church. In this lesson, Dr. Godfrey looks at the history of the Presbyterian church through the Civil War and the changing trajectory of the church in America more broadly.

LESSON OBJECTIVES

1. To survey the vast impact of the Civil War on the church in America
2. To explore the influence of Presbyterians on the intellectual and devotional life of the church
3. To introduce the growing pessimism and embrace of premillennialism

SCRIPTURE READING

You shall remember that you were a slave in the land of Egypt, and the Lord your God brought you out from there with a mighty hand and an outstretched arm.

—Deuteronomy 5:15a

LECTURE OUTLINE

A. Presbyterianism helps us understand what was happening in the religious life of denominations throughout America during the Civil War.
   1. Many American denominations split along North/South lines before the outbreak of the war.
   2. The Presbyterian church managed to stay together until the general assembly of 1861.
      a. Gardiner Springs introduced a resolution committing Presbyterians to do all that they could to support the U.S. federal government.
         i. This was a resolution that was in clear opposition to the South and its succession from the Union.

                ii. Many upheld the view that Christian duty was to support the government and resist rebellion (Rom. 13).
           b. The resolution passed on a vote of 156 to 66 and it split the Presbyterian church.
           c. Charles Hodge strongly disagreed with Gardiner Springs.
                i. Hodge asserted that Scripture did not clearly address the issue of whether a state has the right to secede from the federal union.
      3. Charles Hodge is a good illustration of how difficult church life can be when forced to make decisions in the middle of controversy and struggle.
           a. Hodge was on the losing side of all the major decisions made by the Presbyterian church during his lifetime.
                i. He did not want an Old School/New School split in 1837.
                ii. He did not agree with Gardiner Springs' resolution in 1861.
                iii. He did not want the Old and New School to reunite in 1869.
      4. The Presbyterian church would not reunite along Northern and Southern lines until long after the Civil War.
           a. A strong sentiment for peace caused the New and Old School in the North and the New and Old School in the South to reunite after the Civil War.
           b. The split between Northerners and Southerners would take much longer to mend.
           c. The reluctance to reunite between North and South was common to all of the American denominations that split during this period.

B. American Presbyterianism produced some of the best theologians of the century.
   1. Charles Hodge, Archibald Alexander, Samuel Miller, and A.A. Hodge were influential Princeton theologians.
        a. Charles Hodge was the teacher of systematic theology at Princeton for more than fifty years.
        b. Archibald Alexander always emphasized the need of a renewed heart in his teaching.
        c. Samuel Miller was an expert in preaching and church life.
        d. A.A. Hodge, the son of Charles Hodge, was also a splendid theologian and effective teacher.
        e. People looked to Princeton as a bastion of sound theology.
   2. James Thornwell and Robert Dabney were important Presbyterian theologians in the South.
        a. Robert Dabney firmly believed that the experience of God had to go through the mind as well as the emotions.
             i. He was opposed to Finney's disregard for education, dignity, and orderly worship.
             ii. He believed that excitement and emotions did not necessarily constitute true faith.

C. Presbyterians in the nineteenth century understood music to be of crucial importance for the life of the church.
   1. Music has the ability to dramatically stir the human heart.
      a. Presbyterians wanted vital and refined worship.
   2. *The Voice of Praise* youth hymnal was created in 1872.
      a. Presbyterians believed that bad music was corrupting the sensibilities of the youth.
      b. It became apparent that children did not esteem worship because of the sensational style of music in the Sabbath school.
   3. Robert Dabney opposed instruments in public worship entirely.
      a. He thought that of all the instruments that could be used in worship, the organ would be the worst choice of them all.
   4. Presbyterians' concern for proper worship illustrates the various questions the church in could freely ask during the nineteenth century.

D. Postmillennialism gave Charles Hodge a remarkable amount of optimism throughout all the changes of the Presbyterian church in the nineteenth century.
   1. Hodge never became overly troubled about the various splits occurring in the church, and he was tolerant to an extent that today we might find surprising.
   2. Hodge was a postmillennialist who believed the church would persevere through such splits and divisions only to emerge stronger.
   3. Hodge's postmillennialism was beginning to lose its footing as more Christians were becoming pessimistic.

E. Dispensational premillennialism began to advance in the late nineteenth and early twentieth centuries.
   1. Premillennialism seemed natural to the rising tide of criticism against Christianity.
   2. John Nelson Darby primarily developed dispensational premillennialism.
      a. Plymouth Brethren teaching heavily influenced Darby.
         i. He believed the end was near and that things were only going to get worse.
      b. He believed that Christians would be raptured from the tribulation and Christ would return to establish His millennial kingdom.
         i. During His millennial reign, Christ would fulfill the Old Testament promises to Israel.
   3. Dwight L. Moody embraced premillennialism and it widely increased in popularity and creditability.
      a. The tribulations and the rapture would become the touchstone of orthodoxy in the early twentieth century.
   4. Christians were becoming distressed about the future of the church.

STUDY QUESTIONS

1. Which of the following denominations split along North/South lines during the Civil War?
   a. Presbyterians
   b. Methodists
   c. Baptists
   d. All of the above

2. Charles Hodge was on the losing side of two of the most important decisions the general assembly of the Presbyterian church had to make in the nineteenth century.
   a. True
   b. False

3. Even though it took decades for the Presbyterian church to reunite across North/South lines, the Old School and New School were able to reunite in both the North and South.
   a. True
   b. False

4. The nineteenth-century theologian who was opposed to the introduction of instruments into public worship was _____.
   a. Charles Hodge
   b. A.A. Hodge
   c. Robert Dabney
   d. James Henley Thornwell

5. John Nelson Darby was influenced by the _____ in his development of dispensational premillennialism.
   a. Seventh-day Adventists
   b. Northern Presbyterians
   c. Southern Baptists
   d. Plymouth Brethren

6. Dispensational premillennialists considered the _____ as the touchstone of orthodoxy.
   a. Return of Christ
   b. Tribulation
   c. Millennial reign
   d. Rapture

8—Through the Civil War

DISCUSSION QUESTIONS

1. What does the North/South split of American denominations during the Civil War tell use about the nature of the relationship between the church and culture?

2. The general assembly of the Presbyterian church consistently decided against the judgment of Charles Hodge. Which of the decisions do you believe the general assembly was correct in making? Why?

3. Dabney believed the experience of God had to go through the mind as well as through the emotions. Can you explain the deficiency of experiencing God only through the mind or the emotions alone?

4. Why was postmillennial eschatology losing ground to dispensational premillennialism during the nineteenth century?

9

Christianity & Science

INTRODUCTION

The idea that Christianity is incompatible with science is false. In this lesson, Dr. Godfrey exposes this falsehood by exploring the four major fields of scientific endeavor that were attacking Christianity and contributing to the growing pessimism of the nineteenth century.

LESSON OBJECTIVES

1. To establish a proper relationship between science and Christianity
2. To elaborate on the developments of the nineteenth century that directly attacked the Christian worldview

SCRIPTURE READING

Sovereign Lord, who made the heaven and the earth and the sea and everything in them....

—Acts 4:24b

Who has established all the ends of the earth?

—Proverbs 30:4b

LECTURE OUTLINE

A. Science began to oppose Christianity in the nineteenth century.
   1. Science is one of the main causes for the growing sense of pessimism amongst American Christians.
      a. Christianity and the developments of natural science were seen as compatible until the nineteenth century.
         i. Some of the finest scientists have been Christians.
      b. The notion that Christianity and science must be opposed to each other is false.

i. Christianity has never been the enemy of science and has always promoted the exploration of God's world.
    2. Science declared the war itself between Christianity.
        a. Science was developing in ways that attempted to discount the Christian understanding of the Bible.
        b. Anti-Christian scientists began to use their convictions to oppose Christianity.
    3. Christians believe that science cannot possibly contradict what God has revealed.
        a. Only science that attempts to undermine the Bible is suspect.
        b. The fact that scientific understanding is continually changing should only lead us to humility and a continued exploration of God's world.
            i. We are all part of a finite creation, so our understanding can never truly reach the infinite.
    4. Science began to take on a philosophical component in the nineteenth century.
        a. People were beginning to believe that science could explain what life was all about and came to revere it as the supreme authority.
            i. Christians must ask if science has overstepped its boundaries in this respect.
    5. There are four main areas that began to challenge Christianity during the nineteenth century.

B. Biblical criticism emerges to explain the Bible while challenging the Christian faith.
    1. Biblical criticism seeks to answer how the Bible came to be.
        a. It is interested in how the Bible was put together and by what authors.
    2. Biblical criticism lacks the external evaluation that would be necessary to prove the findings of its various scholars.
        a. Abraham Kuyper recounts an experience as a student at the University of Leiden of unscientific biblical criticism.
            i. A professor taught that the book of John was reliable and written by the Apostle John, yet proclaimed the opposite in a lecture two years later.
        b. Academia would still determine the findings of biblical criticism as definite and certain while viewing conservative scholarship as biased.

C. Darwinism presents a fundamentally different way of understanding human beings.
    1. Charles Darwin published *The Origin of Species by Means of Natural Selection* in 1859 and *The Descent of Man* in 1871.
        a. He began the long effort to prove that human beings arose by natural selection and evolution from lower species.
        b. This directly contradicts the Bible's account of the creation of man and calls into question whether we are created with an immortal soul in the image of God.
    2. The theory of natural selection through the survival of the fittest directly influenced the social movements of the nineteenth and twentieth centuries.

a. Adolf Hitler's worldview was fueled by social Darwinism.
    i. He believed in the superiority of one race over the other.
    ii. He began a program of euthanasia on the handicapped.
3. Darwinism only offers a bleak and deterministic outlook on life.
    a. Darwinism disposes of both God and human freedom.

D. Marxism asserts that economic forces drive the course of human history.
    1. Karl Marx and Frederick Engels published *The Communist Manifesto* in 1848.
        a. It gave birth to the social, political, and economic movement of communism.
    2. Marx published *Das Kapital* in 1867.
        a. Marx believed that history could be understood by economic conflict that would lead to an inevitable future.
            i. Societies follow a revolutionary economic pattern from agriculture to capital, to the overthrow of capital, and finally to the dictatorship of the proletariat.
            ii. A utopia where people shared freedom and wealth equally would soon follow.
        b. People believed Marxism was the solution to poverty and economic inequality.
    3. Joseph Stalin was influenced by Marxist ideology.
        a. Stalin murdered millions more than Hitler in the name of social equality.
            i. This parallels the French Revolution's descent into terror and dictatorship.
    4. Marxism is merely another form of determinism.
        a. Intellectuals in the West would continue to espouse Marxism despite the knowledge of where it leads.
            i. They understood Stalin as caught up in the inevitable process of history.

E. Freudianism directs its focus on the unconscious impulses of the individual.
    1. Freudianism is another manifestation of a deterministic worldview in the nineteenth century.
        a. Sigmund Freud believed that if we could explore the unconscious, we would come to understand the tensions between the *id*, the *ego*, and the *superego*.
            i. These tensions make an individual who they are.
            ii. A person could gain a level of understanding and control by understanding these tensions.
    2. Freudianism is deeply embedded in our culture.
        a. People commonly understand human emotions in Freudian terms.

F. The deterministic worldviews that contributed to the growing pessimism of Christians in the nineteenth century can arm us with an effective historical apologetic for the Christian faith.
   a. People commonly bring up the violence throughout the history of the church as a charge against Christianity.
      i. They still have to account for the millions of people who have died at the hands of deterministic worldviews.

STUDY QUESTIONS

1. The war between Christianity and science was initiated by a Christian understanding that the Bible is incompatible with scientific endeavor.
   a. True
   b. False

2. Freudianism, Marxism, and Darwinism can all be considered _____ philosophies.
   a. Empirical
   b. Rationalistic
   c. Existentialist
   d. Deterministic

3. Biblical criticism has the essential characteristics of a science.
   a. True
   b. False

4. Darwinism calls into question _____.
   a. Creation
   b. Adam and Eve
   c. Man as made in God's image
   d. All of the above

5. Nazism was heavily influenced by _____.
   a. Marxism
   b. Freudianism
   c. Darwinism
   d. All of the above

6. Which of the following is not a part of Marx's pattern for society?
   a. Agriculture
   b. Formation of capital
   c. Overthrow of capital
   d. Dictatorship of the bourgeoisie

DISCUSSION QUESTIONS

1. How can you defend the Christian faith against the presumption that it is antagonistic to science?

2. What is an apt reply to the notion that scholars who defend the Bible are simply prejudiced?

3. How is Freudianism a type of determinism?

4. Dr. Godfrey mentioned the need for an effective historical apologetic for Christianity to confront anti-Christian worldviews. Can you explain this?

10

Roman Catholicism

INTRODUCTION

Roman Catholics reacted to the mounting pressures of the nineteenth century by reasserting papal authority. In this lesson, Dr. Godfrey shows how the declarations of the First Vatican Council create a dilemma for today's Roman Catholic scholar.

LESSON OBJECTIVES

1. To situate the Roman Catholic Church in the context of the nineteenth century
2. To review the decisions of the First Vatican Council
3. To identify the problems that the First Vatican Council creates for Roman Catholics

SCRIPTURE READING

It is a snare to say rashly, "It is holy," and to reflect only after making vows.

—Proverbs 20:25

LECTURE OUTLINE

A. The Roman Catholic Church recovered dramatically from the Reformation.
   1. Rome reorganized at the Council of Trent in the sixteenth century.
      a. A disciplined priesthood, better education, and an emphasis on foreign missions contributed to its growth.
      b. It engaged in mission work primarily in South America, Central America, and Asia.
   2. The papacy and the Roman Catholic Church remained very powerful.
      a. The allegory in *The Pilgrim's Progress* of the papacy as a nearly dead giant was perhaps too optimistic.

B. The Roman Catholic Church faced increasing pressures as two significant areas of Europe were in the process of centralizing.
  1. The process of centralization pulled Germany together as a nation in the latter part of the nineteenth century.
     a. Germany was once a collection of territories governed by a local prince or king.
     b. As Germany centralized, Brandenburg became Prussia, and Prussia became Germany.
     c. Germany sought to eliminate local regional alliances to create one national identity for its people.
  2. The process of centralization in Italy was particularly challenging for the Roman Catholic Church.
     a. King Victor Emmanuel II united the independently governed territories of Italy in 1861.
     b. The Papal States were a roadblock to Victor Emmanuel's efforts to unify Italy.
        i. The papacy exercised political power over the central part of Italy for nearly a thousand years.
        ii. The papacy lost the income, power, and influence of the Papal States.
        iii. It would take the Vatican 150 years to send a delegate to the celebrations of the unification of Italy.
     c. Victor Emmanuel believed Rome was needed as the capital of the newly unified Italy.
        i. He seized the city of Rome in 1870 during the reign of Pope Pius IX.
        ii. The papacy refused to acknowledge the authority of Italy as a nation and feared that even more power would be taken away.
        iii. The popes sequestered themselves in the Vatican from 1870 to 1929.
  3. The Roman Catholic Church was being confronted with the new mentalities developing in Europe.
     a. Modernism, socialism, and Darwinism were challenging Catholics just as they were challenging Protestants.
     b. Italy was beginning to secularize.
        i. The power of the church in society had diminished, though the church was still highly regarded.
        ii. The papacy was greatly alarmed and took a conservative stance in reaction to the pressures of secularization.

C. Pope Pius IX called an ecumenical council to reassert and clarify the power of the papacy.
  1. The First Vatican Council declared the official position of the Roman Catholic Church.
     a. The Roman Catholic Church has determined that ecumenical councils called by the pope are unchangeable.

b. Roman Catholic scholars of today are embarrassed by the decisions of the First Vatican Council.

c. Protestants must remind Roman Catholics that these decisions cannot simply be avoided.

2. The First Vatican Council made many bold claims.

a. It claimed that the purpose of the Vatican Council was only to declare what the church has always believed.

b. It claimed that the pope is the source of all spiritual and temporal power on earth.

c. It claimed that the pope, as the successor of Peter and as Christ's presence on earth, has authority over all churches.

d. It claimed that anyone who believed that the pope was not the head of the church could not be saved.

D. The implications of the Vatican Council's claiming to teach what the church has always believed are devastating.

1. The aim of the Vatican Council was to restate the Council of Trent's statement that the papacy only teaches what the Apostles taught.

a. So when Rome teaches about Mary, purgatory, transubstantiation, or the sacrifice of the Mass, it is claiming that these were received from the Apostles.

i. Historians acknowledge that these Roman Catholic doctrines have developed over time.

ii. Today, Roman Catholics hold to the arguments of John Henry Newman that the seeds of these traditions can be found in the Apostles.

E. The implications of the Roman Catholic Church's declaring that ecumenical councils called by the pope are unchangeable are even more devastating.

1. The First Vatican Council claimed that the pope is "free from all error and blemish of error."

a. Protestants must continue to remind Roman Catholics of these claims.

2. The Roman Catholic Church reacted to the pressures of the nineteenth century by reasserting the power of the papacy.

a. This was troubling to many Roman Catholics in the twentieth century.

STUDY QUESTIONS

1. King _____ unified Italy in 1861.
    a. Victor Emmanuel I
    b. Victor Emmanuel II
    c. Umberto I
    d. Umberto II

2. Pope _____ called the First Vatican Council
   a. Pius VIII
   b. Gregory XVI
   c. Pius IX
   d. Leo XIII

3. Roman Catholics did not face quite the same pressures from modernism that Protestants had been facing.
   a. True
   b. False

4. The political and social changes in Italy prompted Rome to modernize the papacy.
   a. True
   b. False

5. Who can be saved, according to the First Vatican Council?
   a. Protestants
   b. Greek Orthodox
   c. Roman Catholics
   d. All of the above

6. Rome believes that the pope is infallible when he teaches _____.
   a. *Ex nihilo*
   b. *Ex Deo*
   c. *Ex cathedra*
   d. *Ex officio*

DISCUSSION QUESTIONS

1. In what ways did the papacy react similarly to the monarchs in Europe during the periods of radical social change in the nineteenth century?

2. What were some of the reasons that the Vatican was so slow to recognize the unification of Italy?

3. The First Vatican Council maintained the position of the Council of Trent that Rome only teaches what has been handed down from the Apostles. How can this be challenged historically?

4. Why is it important to remind Roman Catholics that the teachings of the First Vatican Council cannot be changed?

11

The Church in Europe

INTRODUCTION

Revival spread throughout Europe by men who faithfully preached the gospel. In this lesson, Dr. Godfrey introduces us to these men and perhaps the most important thinker for the Christian in the modern day, Abraham Kuyper.

LESSON OBJECTIVES

1. To introduce the important figures of the revivals in Geneva, Scotland, and the Netherlands
2. To build a foundation for understanding the importance of Abraham Kuyper through his many achievements

SCRIPTURE READING

Do you see a man skillful in his work? He will stand before kings.
—Proverbs 22:29

LECTURE OUTLINE

A. The First Great Awakening in America led to a significant revival in Scotland that spread throughout Europe through influential preachers.
   1. Robert Haldane was a prominent preacher who emerged from the revival in Scotland and who would greatly influence the revival in Geneva.
      a. Haldane was an educated layman who was concerned about the state of the church.
         i. He was most particularly concerned about spreading the gospel to the unreached parts of the world.
      b. Haldane understood that Geneva had drifted away from orthodoxy and was in need of revival.
         i. He set up a Bible study in the coffee shop across from the seminary in Geneva in 1816.

ii. Haldane's Bible study greatly influenced Merle D'Aubigné.
2. Merle D'Aubigné was a prominent preacher who would go on to influence the revival in the Dutch Reformed Church.
   a. D'Aubigné was a famous writer of the history of the Reformation, but he would become more widely known as a preacher.
   b. D'Aubigné's preaching in the Netherlands continued the work of revival that began in Scotland and spread to Geneva.
3. Thomas Chalmers carried on the revival in Scotland with a concern for the spiritual and social health of the nation.
   a. Chalmers was very concerned for the poor in Glasgow and wanted to improve working conditions for them.
   b. His leadership led to a great renewal in the Church of Scotland that would in turn lead to the Disruption in the Church of Scotland in the 1840s.
      i. The Church in Scotland wanted to be free from excessive control by Parliament.
      ii. The Disruption led to the formation of the Free Church of Scotland.

B. The revival in the Netherlands greatly influenced Dutch society through Guillaume Groen van Prinsterer.
   1. Guillaume Groen van Prinsterer was converted during the revival begun by Merle D'Aubigné.
      a. Initially, the revival in the Netherlands began among the well-educated and influential Dutch who spoke French.
   2. Van Prinsterer was part of the ruling elite of the Netherlands in the nineteenth century.
      a. He was in the cabinet of the king of the Netherlands.
         i. The Kingdom of the Netherlands was established after the Congress of Vienna defeated Napoleon in 1815.
   3. Van Prinsterer was removed from the cabinet after his conversion and was made the archivist for the House of Orange.
      a. He used this as an opportunity to study Dutch history and Calvinism and became convinced that Dutch society needed Calvinism.
   4. Van Prinsterer founded a political party called the Anti-Revolutionary Party.
      a. The name of the party was a reaction to the French Revolution.
         i. Van Prinsterer believed Christians needed to stand against the unbelief and social leveling of the French Revolution.
         ii. Van Prinsterer also believed the condition of the poor and the workers needed improvement.
   5. Van Prinsterer was elected to Parliament.
      a. He was the only Anti-Revolutionary in Parliament, but the movement would soon attract Abraham Kuyper.

11—The Church in Europe

C. Abraham Kuyper is arguably the most important Christian thinker of the modern era.
   1. Kuyper attempted to situate himself in the modern world.
      a. Many Christians longed for the time when Christianity was established in law, but Kuyper understood that Christianity in the West had been disestablished.
   2. Kuyper helps us more than any other modern Christian thinker to understand the situation we are in today.

D. Abraham Kuyper was a man of extraordinary ability who would remarkably influence in the Netherlands during the nineteenth century.
   1. Kuyper was born into a ministerial family in 1837.
      a. He was the son of a minister in the state Reformed church.
         i. His father was orthodox, but he was not active in transforming the life of the church.
         ii. His father would later be called to a church in Leiden, where Kuyper would attend university.
   2. Kuyper heavily studied the works of John Calvin and John á Lasco.
      a. John á Lasco was a Reformer in Poland.
      b. Kuyper's studies laid the foundation for his later career.
   3. Kuyper entered the ministry in 1863.
      a. He was not yet converted and found it very difficult to write sermons.
      b. He had a difficult time reaching the people of the village because they were tired of having unconverted ministers.
         i. He was able to learn more about these people and was so intrigued by their piety that it led to his conversion.
   4. Kuyper began a significant career as a preacher.
      a. He was called from the village church to the city of Utrecht.
      b. He was called from Utrecht to Amsterdam.
      c. It was during this period that he began to write about the need for reform in the Dutch church.
   5. Kuyper decided to leave the ministry in 1874 to pursue a career in politics.
      a. Kuyper believed that there needed to be a Christian presence in the political life of the nation.
      b. He could not serve in Parliament if he was still a minister.
   6. Kuyper devoted himself to an incredible breadth of labors, understanding that ideas needed be put into action through institutions.
      a. He was the editor of two newspapers.
      b. He helped found the Free University of Amsterdam as a member of Parliament and became a professor there.
      c. He helped start a new Reformed denomination and a labor movement.
      d. He would turn the Anti-Revolutionary Party into a mass political party and become the prime minister of the Netherlands.

7. Kuyper was an able communicator.
    a. His ability to communicate was essential to the radical changes he wanted to enact in Dutch society.
        i. He wanted a free nation, a free church, and schools where the children of believers could be educated.

STUDY QUESTIONS

1. The First Great Awakening in America was not influential on the revival that began in Scotland and spread throughout Europe.
    a. True
    b. False

2. A string of revivals that spread throughout Europe was started by _____ in Scotland.
    a. Merle D'Aubigné
    b. Robert Haldane
    c. Thomas Chalmers
    d. Abraham Kuyper

3. There were significant revivals in the nineteenth century in all of the following countries except _____.
    a. Switzerland
    b. Netherlands
    c. Germany
    d. Scotland

4. Guillaume Groen van Prinsterer founded a political party called the _____ Party.
    a. Labour
    b. Revolutionary
    c. Socialist
    d. Anti-Revolutionary

5. Abraham Kuyper was heavily influenced by the ideas of _____.
    a. Martin Luther
    b. John Calvin
    c. John á Lasco
    d. Both b and c

6. Abraham Kuyper began a career in politics immediately after his conversion.
    a. True
    b. False

11—The Church in Europe

DISCUSSION QUESTIONS

1. How does Robert Haldane's study of the Bible in a coffee shop in Geneva help us to understand the priority of Scripture in our own lives?

2. What was the significance behind the name of the political party begun by Guillaume Groen van Prinsterer?

3. Why does Dr. Godfrey consider Abraham Kuyper to be the most important Christian thinker of the modern era?

4. What were the reasons Abraham Kuyper left his career in ministry?

12

Abraham Kuyper

INTRODUCTION

Abraham Kuyper did not ignore the realities that the church faced in the modern world. In this last lesson, Dr. Godfrey maps out Kuyper's vision of a pluralistic society that would not hinder our freedom to be Christians.

LESSON OBJECTIVES

1. To present Abraham Kuyper's central ideas for how Christians are to relate to the world
2. To introduce Kuyper's blueprint for a society that would allow for both diversity and freedom
3. To communicate the importance of Kuyper's thought for Christians in our modern day

SCRIPTURE READING

The natural person does not accept the things of the Spirit of God.

—1 Corinthians 2:14a

Please let us go three days' journey into the wilderness that we may sacrifice to the Lord our God.

—Exodus 5:3b

LECTURE OUTLINE

A. Abraham Kuyper insisted that answering the fundamental question about the type of world we live in would help Christians navigate modern challenges.
   1. Do we live in a world that is normal or abnormal?
      a. If an evolutionist worldview is true, then all of the problems in this world are normal and what we would expect to find.

           i. Sickness and death are perfectly normal.
           ii. Social injustice at the hands of a merely evolving species is the way of the world.
        b. If the Christian worldview is true, then Christians must assert that the world in which we live is entirely abnormal.
           i. We live in a fallen world, and we have to understand that we are in pursuit of something far better.
           ii. In this world, death is fundamentally abnormal; it is not natural.
     2. How then should the Christian view death?
        a. Death is the last enemy.
           i. Christ defeated death on our behalf, and we look forward to a day in which we will be glorified with Him.
        b. If death is unnatural, then certainly a worldview that exploits the weak unto death is unnatural as well.
           i. Kuyper was almost prophetic in that Darwinism would be the worldview that fueled the Nazi agenda.

B. Abraham Kuyper insisted that understanding how Christians are different from the world will help us to understand our place in the world.
    1. Christians are different because of the regenerating work of God in our hearts.
       a. The way we live our lives should then be different.
       b. Our sanctification should spill over into the world around us.
    2. Christians think differently from non-Christians.
       a. It is not at all surprising that non-Christians do not understand the way Christians think—the Spirit of God has not regenerated them.
       b. Christians should then be free to pursue knowledge of the world in a way that is Christian.
    3. Christians are antithetical to the world.
       a. Christians are called to live peaceably in this world, yet there is a spiritual battle that places us at odds with the world.

C. Abraham Kuyper insists that common grace is the only way to explain how the world, in antithesis to the Christian, is able to do anything that resembles good.
    1. God has preserved the unregenerate by His common grace.
       a. Non-Christians are able to do skillful work and create beautiful things.
       b. The good things that non-Christians are able to do are not from some inherent good that they possess, but from God's common grace.
    2. Thomas Aquinas divided the world into nature and grace in order to account for the accomplishments of the unregenerate.
       a. Thomas believed that there was some part of nature that was not completely fallen that allowed for such great accomplishments by unbelievers.
       b. Kuyper properly understood the extent of the fall and believed that God's preserving work has kept people from being as bad as they could be.

D. Abraham Kuyper insisted that the sovereignty of spheres is the only way to protect against tyranny in the modern world.
   1. Throughout Western history, there has always been a struggle between the state and the church for domination.
      a. The church was clearly losing influence as a social power in the nineteenth century.
      b. Kuyper believed the greatest problem the Western world would have to face was state control of every facet of life.
         i. Kuyper anticipated the tendencies of European society that would later manifest themselves in fascism and communism.
         ii. Kuyper also understood that the legal reestablishment of Christianity was no longer an option in the modern world.
   2. Kuyper believed the answer to state control was to recognize that God created the world with a variety of spheres under His direct authority.
      a. God did not give the state all power in society.
         i. The state exists to administer justice in society.
      b. God created other spheres in society, like the family, that are directly accountable to Him.
         i. The state did not create the family, and God did not give children to the state.
         ii. God gave children to the family, and the family is responsible for how children are raised.
         iii. The state's right to administer justice extends to the protection of children from harm, but the state does not have the authority to raise children.
      c. Kuyper's vision has radical implications for the education of children.
         i. The state does not have the authority to decide how children will be educated—parents hold such authority.
         ii. The state should then support the freedom of parents to send their children to the schools they see fit.
      d. Kuyper believed that genuine pluralism was the key to genuine freedom.
         i. A modern society necessitates a variety of churches for a variety of families for a variety of schools for a variety of political parties.
         ii. These spheres would function to preserve a genuine diversity and a genuine freedom.

E. Abraham Kuyper's ideas can be incredibly useful in America today.
   1. Kuyper attempted to provide a pluralistic model that would actually allow for a plurality of ideas.
      a. Christians are often thought to be antagonistic to a pluralistic society because they believe they alone worship the one true God.
         i. Kuyper's model allows Christians to live without compromising the truth or a commitment to evangelism.

12—Abraham Kuyper

          ii. The freedom envisioned at the core of Kuyper's model allows people to live in accordance with their beliefs.
      b. The radical individualism of America is truly at the heart of the increasing intolerance we see today.
          i. Every individual demands to be equally respected in every institution.
   2. Abraham Kuyper insisted that the sphere of science and advanced thought is where the university should exist.
      a. The university needs to exist in its own sphere if it is to remain free.
          i. It is not under the authority of the state, the church, or the family.
          ii. Universities are the gathering place of likeminded thinkers to promote advanced thought.

F. Abraham Kuyper's thought not only provides Christians with a blueprint for the modern world; it also provides us with a hope that rests ultimately in God.
   1. Kuyper would have a profound effect on Reformed theology.
      a. He greatly influenced Herman Bavinck and many other biblical scholars.
   2. Kuyper's accomplishments in the Netherlands would only last fifty to seventy years.
      a. The dominance of modern thought would eventually erode the Christian convictions, institutions, and experiences that Kuyper was instrumental in creating.
      b. This points us to our lasting hope in, and leads us in prayer to, the Sovereign Lord and an understanding that all our accomplishments are ultimately by His grace.

STUDY QUESTIONS

1. Death is considered _____ in a Christian worldview.
    a. Natural
    b. Normal
    c. Abnormal
    d. Both a and b

2. The theologian who divided the world into nature and grace to account for the accomplishments of the unregenerate was _____.
    a. Abraham Kuyper
    b. Augustine
    c. Thomas Aquinas
    d. John Calvin

3. Abraham Kuyper's idea that there are spheres directly accountable to God is called sphere of _____.
   a. Autonomy
   b. Diversity
   c. Separation
   d. Sovereignty

4. Abraham Kuyper understood common grace as God's way of extending saving grace to the unregenerate.
   a. True
   b. False

5. Abraham Kuyper believed that the dangers facing Western society were authoritative tyranny and _____.
   a. Anarchy
   b. Communism
   c. Individualism
   d. None of the above

6. Abraham Kuyper believed that Christianity could not survive in a pluralistic society.
   a. True
   b. False

DISCUSSION QUESTIONS

1. How is the evolutionist's view of death at odds with Christianity?

2. How does Abraham Kuyper's view of common grace take total depravity into deeper consideration than Thomas Aquinas' view of a world divided into nature and grace?

3. How is radical individualism manifesting itself in America today? Do you think Abraham Kuyper's ideas could provide a solution?

4. Much in the same way that the accomplishments of Abraham Kuyper would only last fifty to seventy years, cultural influences continue to erode Christian convictions today. What posture should we assume as Christians?

Answer Key for Study Questions

Lesson 1
1. a
2. b
3. d
4. b
5. b
6. c

Lesson 2
1. b
2. d
3. c
4. b
5. a
6. d

Lesson 3
1. b
2. b
3. c
4. a
5. d
6. c

Lesson 4
1. b
2. c
3. d
4. b
5. d
6. b

Lesson 5
1. b
2. b
3. c
4. d
5. d
6. b

Lesson 6
1. c
2. b
3. b
4. d
5. d
6. b

Lesson 7
1. b
2. c
3. b
4. b
5. b
6. c

Lesson 8
1. d
2. b
3. a
4. c
5. d
6. d

Lesson 9
1. b
2. d
3. b
4. d
5. c
6. d

Lesson 10
1. b
2. c
3. b
4. b
5. c
6. c

Lesson 11
1. b
2. b
3. c
4. d
5. d
6. b

Lesson 12
1. c
2. c
3. d
4. b
5. c
6. b